3|01

23.⁵⁴

NATURE'S FURY

VOLCANOES

Cari Meister

Visit us at
www.abdopub.com

Published by ABDO Publishing Company, 4940 Viking Drive, Edina, MN 55435.

Printed in the United States.

Edited by: Paul Joseph
Art Direction: John Hamilton
Contributing Editor: Morgan Hughes

Cover photo: DigitalVision
Interior photos: DigitalVision, pages 1, 3-5, 7, 8, 11, 13-15, 18, 19, 30, 31
                 AP/Wide World Photos, pages 21-23
                 Corbis, pages 24-28
                 NASA/JPL, page 10

Sources: Bondar, Barbara. *Volcano! Dome of Fire.* Logan, Iowa: Perfection Learning Corporation, 1997; Lane, Frank W. *The Violent Earth.* Topsfield, Massachusetts: Salem House, 1986; Laskin, David. *Braving the Elements: The Stormy History of American Weather.* New York: Doubleday, 1996; Robinson, Andrew. *Earth Shock.* New York: Thames and Hudson, Ltd, 1993; Various articles on *http://nationalgeographic.com*; Wood, Dr. Robert Muir. *Earthquakes and Volcanoes: Causes, Effects & Predictions.* New York: Weidenfeld & Nicolson, 1987.

Library of Congress Cataloging–in–Publication Data

Meister, Cari.
   Volcanoes / Cari Meister
      p. cm. — (Nature's fury)
   Includes index.
   Summary: Discusses the nature, causes, and dangers of volcanoes, volcanoes of the past, and ways to survive them.
   ISBN 1-57765-084-0
   1. Volcanoes—Juvenile literature. [1. Volcanoes] I. Title. II. Series: Meister, Cari. Nature's fury.
   QE521.3.M45 1999
   551.21—dc21
                           98-15730
                                CIP
                                 AC

CONTENTS

VOLCANOES

LONG AGO, ROMANS WORSHIPPED A GOD CALLED VULCAN. Vulcan was the god of fire. He was in charge of making other gods' weapons. Romans believed that Vulcan worked in a forge under an island in the Mediterranean Sea. They named the island Vulcano.

The Romans believed that when Vulcan was pounding arrows and swords, flames from his forge would spew right out the top of the island! Hot red rivers would pour down the sides of the mountain. Ash and smoke would rise up and fill the skies. To the Romans this meant stay away! Today, if you saw a volcano erupt, you would stay away, too! But today, we know that it's not Vulcan creating the eruptions. Volcanoes are a natural process that start deep down inside the earth.

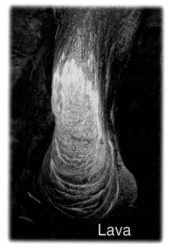

Lava

Think of the earth as a golf ball. The golf ball's hard outer shell is not the same as the inner core. The earth is not the same throughout, either. The earth is made up of three layers. The top layer is called the crust. The crust is located just below the oceans and land. The crust is rocky. The layer below the crust is the mantle. The mantle is very hot. It's so hot that some of the rocks melt. Melted rock below the earth's surface is called magma. Underneath the mantle is the core. The core is solid metal. It stays solid

A volcano erupts.

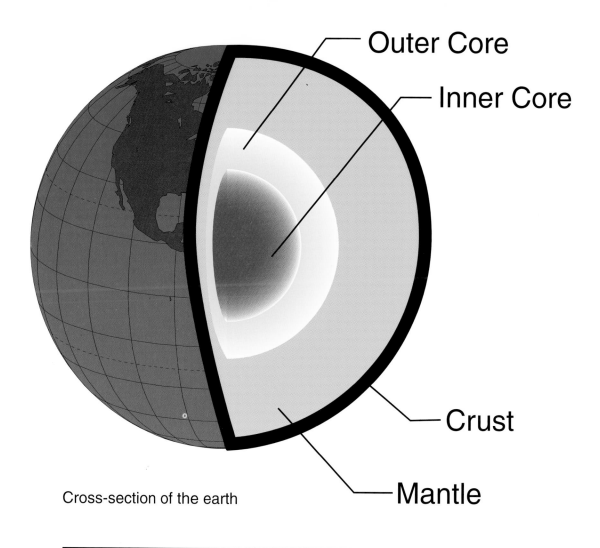

Outer Core

Inner Core

Crust

Mantle

Cross-section of the earth

because of great pressure. The core has two parts: the inner core and the outer core.

Let's go back to the outer layer again, the crust. The crust is broken up into several large pieces called plates. The plates are thousands of miles across. They fit together sort of like a jigsaw puzzle. Plates float like rafts on top of the mantle's melted rock.

Plates are always on the move. But they don't move fast. Some plates move about two to three inches (5 to 7.6 cm) a year. Some plates only move one inch (2.54 cm) in 100 years. When plates move, they carry whatever is on top of them. Some plates carry entire oceans! They also carry continents and islands. As the plates move, they bump into each other.

Sometimes they pass each other sideways. Sometimes they drift apart. When plates push against each other, pressure builds. When the pressure is finally relieved, we feel an earthquake.

Some places along the crust, especially near the edges of plates, are weak. Holes and cracks form near these weak spots. Underneath the plates, magma is always moving. Sometimes magma makes its way through the holes and cracks to the earth's surface where it bubbles up a long tube. It bubbles and bubbles until it reaches the hole at the top of the tube and erupts! Magma oozes out of the hole, or crater. The instant it spills from the crater, it's called lava.

When magma finds a new place on the earth's surface to escape, a volcano is born. However, most of the time magma escapes through volcanoes that have been around for hundreds of thousands of years.

Hot rock from deep within the earth bursts to the surface.

VOLCANOES: WHERE ARE THEY?

VOLCANOES ARE FOUND IN MANY PARTS OF THE WORLD. They are found on land. They are also found on the ocean floor. There are over 500 active volcanoes in the world. An active volcano is a volcano that has erupted in the last 10,000 years and that scientists think will erupt again at any time.

A dormant volcano is a volcano that is "sleeping." In other words, dormant volcanoes are volcanoes that have been inactive for a very long time, but that are likely to erupt sometime in the future. An extinct volcano is a volcano that scientists don't think will ever erupt again. Sometimes scientists are wrong. On the average, one "extinct" volcano erupts about every five years.

One area of the world has more volcanoes than any other. This area

An active volcano

is called the Ring of Fire. It is a big loop that follows the boundary of the Pacific Ocean Plate. Active volcanoes in Japan, South America, Alaska, the Philippines, and Mexico all fall in the Ring of Fire. Japan has close to 80 volcanoes. Chile has 75. The Aleutian Islands and Alaska have about 70 volcanoes.

Volcanoes form where they do because of the location of the plates. Sometimes when two plates push up against each other, the edge of one plate dives underneath the other

RING OF FIRE

plate. This process is called subduction. The plate underneath melts. The molten rock, magma, flows through cracks and erupts on the surface as a volcano.

Some volcanoes form at rifts. Rifts are places where plates have moved apart, leaving deep cracks and spaces. Magma from deep inside the earth seeps up through the cracks. When it makes its way to the surface it's a volcano. Iceland and East Africa have the most rift volcanoes. Together, they have over 160 active rift volcanoes!

Some volcanoes form over hot spots. Scientists believe that long ago, huge meteorites hit the earth, forming hot spots. The meteorites hit the earth's surface so hard that they cracked the plate and damaged the mantle. Today, the cracks allow magma to seep through the damaged spots.

Under the ocean, there are hundreds of hot spots. Volcanoes form over these hot spots, too. At first we can't always see them, because they are hidden underwater. A lot of the time we don't notice an underwater volcano until it sticks up out of the water. Some islands are actually gigantic volcanoes! Hawaii formed over a hot spot. Many of the Hawaiian Islands are actually volcanoes.

Earth is not the only planet to have volcanoes. So far scientists have discovered volcanoes on Mars and Venus. Scientists believe that Olympus Mons, on Mars, is the largest volcano in our entire solar system. Olympus Mons is more than 15 miles (24 km) high and nearly 400 miles (644 km) across!

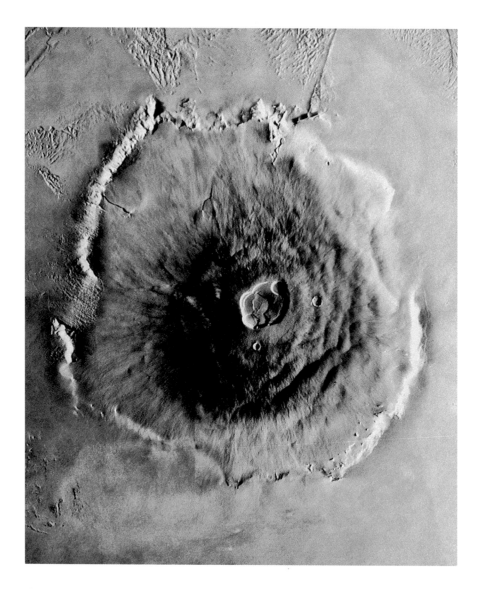

Olympus Mons on the planet Mars, as seen by a Viking orbiter spacecraft in 1976.

TYPES OF VOLCANOES

ALL VOLCANOES ARE DIFFERENT. SOME ERUPT REGULARLY every 10 to 15 years. Others erupt once every 150 to 200 years. Some volcanoes spurt rivers of red lava. When Hawaii's Mauna Loa—the tallest volcano in the world—erupts, long streams of lava flow down the mountain. Other volcanoes don't spurt lava. Some volcanoes cover entire towns in deadly black clouds.

On May 8, 1902, Mount Pelée shot hot gas and debris into the air. A black cloud of ash fell on the city of St. Pierre, on the island of Martinique. The burning gases killed over 30,000 people, the town's entire population.

Volcanologists, people who study volcanoes, divide volcanoes up into four shapes. The shape of a volcano tells how it was formed. A volcano's shape is also a good indicator of what type of eruption to expect. A shield volcano is a volcano with a wide top. Mauna Loa and Mauna Kea in Hawaii are both shield volcanoes. Thin, runny lava called pahoehoe (pa-hoy-hoy) commonly runs down the sides of shield volcanoes during eruptions. Hot pahoehoe lava usually travels about one yard (91cm) per minute. However, if there is a lot of lava and the volcano's slope is steep, it can move 14 miles per hour (22.5 kph). One observer

Pahoehoe lava

described pahoehoe lava like this: "Watching a pahoehoe flow creep and sizzle across a lawn toward a doomed house is like watching a huge snake slowly and relentlessly approaching its prey."

When pahoehoe lava cools, it forms smooth rope-like or billowy pillow shapes. You can walk over cooled pahoehoe lava. Pahoehoe lava occurs when eruptions have very high temperatures. Shield volcanoes can also cause aa lava to form. Aa lava is sharper when it dries. Aa lava does not move like pahoehoe. Aa moves in surges.

Shield volcanoes erupt frequently. They're usually not very violent. With each eruption, lava hardens around the volcano, making it bigger and bigger. Shield volcanoes eventually become massive mountains.

A dome volcano is a steep-sided volcano that looks like a dome. Dome volcanoes form when thick magma pushes up underneath rock. When they erupt, they become plugged with hardened lava. Magma gases build up and build up until the dome finally bulges under the pressure. Watch out! Sometimes, dome volcanoes "blow their tops." Debris from the volcano's side breaks into blocks. The blocks flow down the thick lava, plowing over anything in their way. A dome volcano is usually shorter right after it "blows its top."

Composite volcanoes are the most common type of volcanoes. In an eruption, they first spit out ash, cinder, and hot rocks. That's not all. Next comes the lava. Then more ash. Then more lava. Magma inside a composite volcano heats rocks and water, producing hot steam and rocks. The hot steam makes the magma frothy. It splatters as if you were throwing a milk shake against a wall.

Cinder cone volcanoes form quickly. A cinder cone volcano in Mexico grew to be 500 feet (152 m) in only a couple of days! Cinder cones form when hot cinder and rocks escape from holes in the ground. They usually spurt out lava, but the gases change the lava into small pieces before it hits the ground. The lava pieces fall to the ground as ash and cinders.

Lava from a shield volcano in Hawaii
spills into the Pacific Ocean.

PREDICTING ERUPTIONS

VOLCANOLOGISTS TRY TO PREDICT WHEN VOLCANOES will erupt. They study all kinds of volcanoes. The more volcanoes they study, the more likely they are to predict when a volcano will erupt.

They study dormant and extinct volcanoes to learn what happens after a volcano has erupted. They also study active volcanoes—while they are erupting! A volcanologist's job is risky. Volcanologists walk right into a volcano's crater to take samples! When lava is rolling down hills, they are there to measure temperatures. When dangerous gases threaten towns, they are there to help evacuate people. Many volcanologists have come too close to erupting volcanoes. Many have died by fire, invisible gases and other volcanic accidents.

An eruption

Volcanologists are always monitoring volcanoes. They run water tests. They measure rock temperatures. They analyze pictures. Volcanologists know all about a volcano when it is inactive. This way, when something strange shows up, they are able to quickly spot the problem. The quicker they know that something is up, the quicker they can warn people that a volcano is waking.

Volcanologists use many different tools. They use satellites, tiltmeters, gas samplers, and other scientific tools. Satellites in space

Volcanologists study an erupting volcano.

take pictures. Some remote sensing instruments can actually find and measure magma 20 feet (6 m) underground! If it looks as if a lot of magma is building up under a volcano, volcanologists might predict an eruption. Tiltmeters measure swelling inside the earth. Gas samplers measure what kinds of gases are in the air. An airplane flies over a volcano's vent with special instruments to pick up a gas sample. If the sample shows an increase in sulfur, or a decrease in water vapor, the volcano may be close to erupting.

Some volcanoes spit out bits of steam and rock before they erupt. But sometimes volcanoes spit out steam and rock, and then don't erupt at all. Volcanologists run special tests on rocks that volcanoes throw. The rocks tell us what might happen. Volcanologists look at a rock's magnetic strength. When rocks get warmer, they lose their magnetism. When rocks lose their magnetism, it means that magma is moving. An eruption may be on its way.

Volcanologists also test water and ice around a volcano's vent.

Inside a Volcano

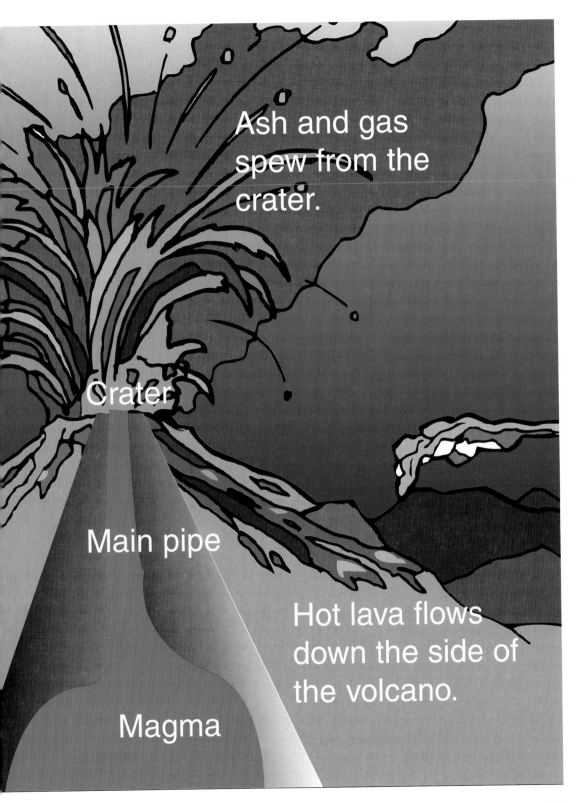

Ash and gas spew from the crater.

Crater

Main pipe

Hot lava flows down the side of the volcano.

Magma

A river of lava.

Water turns to steam when magma heats it. Chunks of ice melt as hot ash pours over them.

Once volcanoes start, they can't be stopped. Volcanologists study a volcano's history to help figure what might happen if it were to erupt again. What direction will the lava flow? Is it likely that the volcano will produce a mudflow? How far will the lava travel? Are any cities or towns in danger?

A volcanologist's tests do not give all of the answers. The earth is always changing. A change in temperature of volcanic rock may mean an eruption, but it may mean something else. Volcanologists do their best in predicting eruptions. But the dynamic earth continually surprises them, as it did in 1980 at Mount St. Helens.

Lava destroys a house in Hawaii.

MOUNT ST. HELENS

MOUNT ST. HELENS IS LOCATED IN WASHINGTON STATE. It's part of the Cascade Mountains. For over 100 years, Mount St. Helens was a beautiful snow-capped mountain. People from all over the world admired its majestic slopes. They considered Mount St. Helens peaceful and solid. Scientists knew better. Scientists knew that Mount St. Helens was really a volcano. Scientists knew that at some time Mount St. Helens would erupt again. They just didn't know when.

In March 1980, Mount St. Helens began to stir. Small earthquakes rumbled under the mountain. A new crater opened at the top. Magma deep below the earth's surface was making its way up inside the volcano. The hot magma heated up water and other materials. The volcano started to spit bits of old ash and rock. Nothing major yet, so scientists ran tests. They looked at the gases coming from the vent. The tests showed little signs of sulfur. If the tests showed a lot of sulfur, the scientists would have thought more about the big eruption to come. But, at this point, they weren't worried.

In April and May, the small eruptions decreased, but the mountain was changing. The whole northern part of the mountain was bulging. It bulged about five feet (1.5 m) per day! Inside the mountain, magma was rising. The force of the magma was pushing the mountain apart. Pressure inside the mountain increased and increased until it erupted.

Mount St. Helens erupts.

On May 18, an earthquake set off the volcano with an explosion equal to 27,000 atomic bombs. The whole northern part of the mountain fell. It crumbled down the side of the mountain, pulling along everything in its way.

A huge avalanche of rock, ice, and mud tumbled down the mountain's side. Ash and hot gas shot through the air—sideways! At the same time, a cloud of ash and gas shot straight up from the volcano's top. The volcano spewed gas and ash into the air for nine hours. Day turned into night. Whole forests fell. Mudflows wrenched out steel bridges. When the eruption finally stopped, part of the mountain was gone. Today, an enormous crater reminds us of Mount St. Helens' power.

The eruption caused a lot of damage. Nearly 130,000 acres of forest was destroyed. That's enough to build 250,000 homes! Millions of birds, mammals, and fish were killed. Tragically, 60 people died. Mount St. Helens is in a remote area. Not many people live in its path. If Mount St. Helens were outside a large city, the story would have been much more devastating.

The wind carried millions of tons of ash around the globe. The ash clogged cars, stalled airplanes, and made it difficult to breathe. Some people suffered from *pneumonoultramicroscopicsilicovolcanoconiosis*. Did you get that? It's one of the longest words in the English language! It's a disease caused by inhaling bad air.

Places around the volcano were covered in ash. Some places near the volcano had four feet (1.2 m) of ash on the ground! Montana, 500 miles (805 km) to the east, had half an inch (1.3 cm) of ash on the ground. People said the ash made the land look like the moon.

Above & Facing page: A logger walks across a fallen tree, one of millions felled by the eruption.

Facing page inset: Mount St. Helens today, as seen from the new Johnston Ridge Observatory.

MOUNT VESUVIUS

VOLCANOES ARE TRICKY. SOMETIMES THEY LOOK LIKE beautiful green mountains. People build homes near them. People build cities near them. The cities may live in peace for hundreds of years. Or they may not. Today, at least 500 million people live close enough to volcanoes for their lives to be in danger from eruptions.

Two thousand years ago, Mount Vesuvius, in southern Italy, was a beautiful green mountain. People knew that it was a volcano. But they thought it was dead. It wasn't. It was only sleeping. On August 24, 79 A.D., Mount Vesuvius woke up. People were already going about their day. The bakers were baking. The shoemakers were making shoes. People were shopping. All of a sudden an earthquake shook the ground. In a matter of seconds the top of Mount Vesuvius tore open. Glowing ash spewed from the giant vent. Ash and mud poured on the cities of Pompeii and Herculaneum. In Pompeii, people choked to death on the fumes. In Herculaneum, mudslides buried people alive. The eruption killed thousands of

Mount Vesuvius erupts.

A cast of a human body in Pompeii, a victim of Mount Vesuvius.

people. Mud and ash completely buried the two towns.

Pompeii and Herculaneum were not discovered until 1,700 years later. When scientists found them they were thrilled. The cities were preserved. Scientists found loaves of bread left in ovens. They found bowls of nuts on kitchen tables. They could even see where people had fallen. They could read the peoples' facial expressions!

Ash from the volcano preserved the cities. After Mount Vesuvius erupted, heavy rains fell on the ash. The rains caused the ash to turn into cement. Over the years, soft things like human bodies decomposed. Hard things like buildings remained. The soft things left behind their shapes. Scientists made casts of the soft things by pouring plaster into the shapes the soft things left in the hardened ash. When they took the plaster out, they could see the shapes of the original things.

Scientists were excited to find Pompeii because it tells us how people lived long ago. Pompeii shows us what buildings looked like, what people ate, and what things were important to them. Today, parts of the Pompeii ruins are open to tourists. People from all over the world like to look at what it was like for the people of Pompeii long ago.

In the past 2,000 years, Mount Vesuvius has erupted more than 50 times, most recently in 1944. Today, scientists watch it closely. It will erupt again. It's only a matter of time.

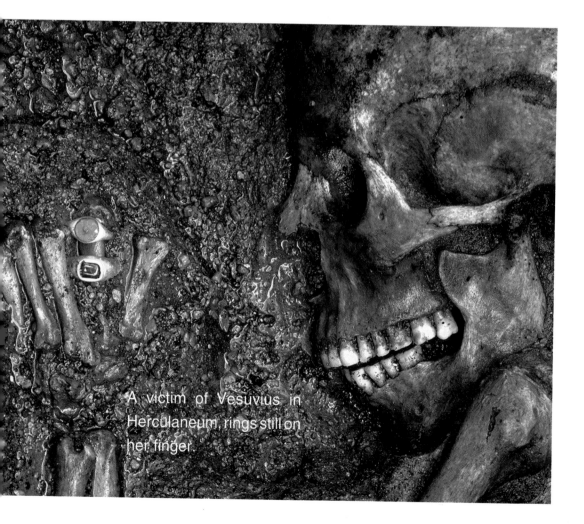

A victim of Vesuvius in Herculaneum, rings still on her finger.

HELPFUL STUFF FROM VOLCANOES

VOLCANOES CAUSE MILLIONS OF DOLLARS IN DAMAGE. They can bury towns. They can kill people, animals, and trees. On the other hand, volcanoes also bring many good things. In fact, some people *want* volcanoes to erupt. A group of people in Papua, New Guinea, perform special dances thought to bring on eruptions.

A volcano throws out ash, lava, and rock. These are all helpful to humans. Ash makes soil fertile, helping crops grow. All over the world, farm land surrounds volcanoes. In Sicily, a volcanic island in the Mediterranean, farmers grow orange and lemon trees. Many tropical fruits like bananas grow in the Canary Islands. The Canary Islands, located off Africa, have many volcanic mountains. Thin layers of ash are most helpful to farmers. Thick layers of ash can mix with rain to create mudslides. Even if a volcano does not erupt in a farmer's lifetime, the farmer benefits from rich soil left from the last eruption.

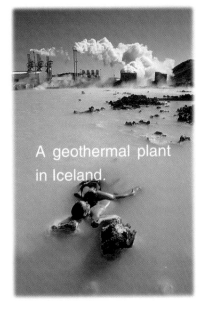

A geothermal plant in Iceland.

Volcanoes spit out many different kinds of rocks. One rock, called pumice, is used in beauty aids. Pumice is very light. It even floats on water! Pumice is used by some people to rub away rough spots on their feet. Pumice is also used in toothpaste. When lava cools quickly it forms obsidian. Obsidian looks like black glass. Obsidian is used for making tools and arrowheads.

Volcanoes can also throw out valuable metals and gemstones. Sapphires and zircons, buried in layers of rock, sometimes come out of the earth with an eruption. Copper, silver, and gold have also been found in volcanic rock. Really valuable gems, like diamonds, are rare. But they have been found. In South Africa, diamonds were found in rocks called kimberlite. Kimberlite rock formed inside volcanoes many years ago.

In some countries, people use the power of volcanoes even before they erupt. Some countries tap into the hot rock that is under volcanoes. In Iceland, heat from lava beds is pumped right into people's homes. In some places, hot rocks heat water underground. The heated water is also pumped right into people's homes. This kind of energy is very clean. It does not pollute the environment.

Over millions of years, volcanoes have changed the earth's landscape. Volcanoes have brought us beautiful mountains and lakes. Some volcanoes form calderas. A caldera is a big basin in the ground. It forms when a volcano falls into the ground after an eruption.

Crater Lake, Oregon

Sometimes calderas fill with water and become lakes. Mount Mazama erupted in 4,600 B.C. Most of the mountain was destroyed. What remained fell into its own empty magma chamber. It filled with water and formed a lake—Crater Lake. It is six miles (9.7 km) wide and 4,000 feet (1,219 m) deep! You can visit Crater Lake in Oregon.

INTERNET SITES

http://volcano.und.nodak.edu

Go to KIDS. Get ideas for school volcano projects or build your own volcano online.

http://www.jason8.eds.com

FIRE & ICE homepage. Check out the Java Case Studies to see volcano photographs.

http://www.nationalgeographic.com

Search the database for information about volcanoes. This site includes stuff on volcanoes from all over the world!

These sites are subject to change. Go to your favorite search engine and type in "volcanoes" for more sites.

PASS IT ON

Science buffs: educate readers around the country by passing on information you've learned about volcanoes. Share your little-known facts and interesting stories. We want to hear from you!

To get posted on the ABDO Publishing Company Web site, E-mail us at "Science@abdopub.com"

Visit the ABDO Publishing Company Web site at:
www.abdopub.com

GLOSSARY

Aa: A type of lava that moves in surges and forms sharp, jagged rocks when dried.

Active volcano: A volcano that has erupted in the last 10,000 years, and will erupt again.

Avalanche: A large mass of snow, ice, earth, or other material that moves down a mountain very fast.

Caldera: A giant crater created when a volcano collapses.

Cinder: A piece of ash.

Cinder cone volcano: A volcano that builds up a mountain of cinder and other rock around its vent.

Composite volcano: A volcano formed when rock chunks and lava spew from a vent.

Crater: The top of a volcano.

Decompose: When something rots.

Dome volcano: A volcano that builds a rounded mountain of soil and rock. They sometimes burst open, spilling thick lava.

Dormant volcano: A volcano that hasn't erupted in many thousands of years, and may or may not erupt again.

Extinct volcano: A volcano that hasn't erupted for more than 10,000 years, and is not expected to erupt again.

Hot spots: Breaks in the earth's crust where magma seeps out.

Lava: Magma that reaches the earth's surface.

Magma: Hot liquid rock inside the earth.

Pahoehoe: A type of lava that forms rope-like rock when dry.

Plates: Sections of the earth's crust.

Preserve: To keep from destruction.

Shield volcano: A volcano that builds a wide, non-steep mountain of runny lava.

Volcano: A vent in the earth's surface where molten rock escapes.

Volcanologists: People who study volcanoes.

INDEX